Aporia

Aporia

John Kinsella

Turtle Point Press
Brooklyn, New York

Turtle Point Press, 208 Java Street, Fifth Floor,
Brooklyn, NY 11222
info@turtlepointpress.com

Library of Congress Cataloguing-in-Publication Data
Names: Kinsella, John, 1963- author.
Title: Aporia / John Kinsella.
Identifiers: LCCN 2025004370 (print) | LCCN 2025004371 (ebook) | ISBN
9781885586285 (paperback) | ISBN 9781885983237 (ebook)
Subjects: LCGFT: Poetry.
Classification: LCC PR9619.3.K55 A75 2025 (print) | LCC PR9619.3.K55
(ebook) | DDC 821/.914--dc23/eng/20250404
LC record available at https://lccn.loc.gov/2025004370
LC ebook record available at https://lccn.loc.gov/2025004371

Design by Joan Wong

Paperback ISBN: 978-1-885586-28-5
eBook ISBN: 978-1-885983-23-7

First Edition
Printed in the United States of America

Contents

FUNERAL

My father said in my dream
        that it was good his funeral
        brought the family together,
and though I wasn't there,
I got what he meant. We see
        deepest through metaphor,
        whose tomography
is a cross section of shadows.
There's an operator's manual
        for poetry about metrics
        and form, a rhyming
dictionary stuck in the back,
but the afterlife seems indifferent
        to 'craft' and doesn't judge
        silhouettes. Dad was so precise
with his mechanics, with his
tools and detailing, that shadow-
        mapping and shadow volume
        telling more of the story
than the originating object or scene.

THE DEMIMONDE OF KANGAROOS

has shifted from the half-light
    of evening & that expanding light
    just before dawn, to mid-afternoons
of a contracting year. If I was inclined

towards appropriation without
    offering a context, I would say something
    like: It's a *rubáiyát* of cloud cover
& freshly risen oat-grass, a gathering coolness,

&, brazenly, a comfort in our presence.
    Or an over-familiarity. And it's not only
    a case of *the same mob* — others' mobs
seem to be precipitating into the lean-to valley,

    altering circadian rhythms & renovating
their senses. In this demimonde of kangaroos.

KANGAROOS GRAZING IN FOG

A calm confidence where ears prick
        but with less edginess —
a noise absorbed into the safety
and comfort of mist. Reading into it?
        Well, if so, I read into 'it'
most days, and their behaviour
is different. My behaviour is different,
        under different conditions.
A morning after the solstice has divided
the world again, and threats of nuclear
        annihilation in the northern
hemisphere insist the southern
is part of the endgame. That brutal
        cliché, *the fog of war*,
which is everything to do with kangaroos,
and fog sitting in the valley seeming
        to create a temporary
refuge to soften the threat, the blows.

PHASING IN & OUT

Only a vivisector
would find the bush
romantic. Looking
out over the valley
and its feeder
valley-ettes, I
am awestruck
by the suspect
nature of my
perceptions.
Close to my feet
in the thin layer
of sand over clay
there is a perfect
sweep, a half-moon,
a windscreen wiper
arc twice over
with lines where
grit or leaves
have stuck under
the blade and left
curves within curves
with machine precision.

But it's not, as no
machine has been here
and car metaphors
squelch hope, a particulate
of an idea where
the air at least
seems clean to breathe.
No, no... thinking it over,
I'd say a kangaroo's tail as it swishes
on thin, cool sand
under a shade tree —
arc as perfect as evergreen
leaves falling and being
swept back & forth,
perfect as all animals
have perfect shapes,
divisors of *fons*
et origo and its
impositions.

Phasing in & out,
late in the day
when mosquitoes
will come if they
are coming, with
haphazard flights;
intent with
purpose.

KANGAROOS GRAZING IN SMOKE

The smothered world
away from flames
how long away from
flames prescribed
as if the atmosphere
requests as if particles
suspended are lapses
in time of planetary
breathing the choke
hold the kangaroos
grazing level to level
to find clean air the
low grass of a season
theoretically beyond
fires coated with
the grazing of land
beyond whose after-
taste brought to the door
brought to blur sun
russet taking warning
taking alert to move on
but where smoke is
all-encompassing, so,
grazing on the way
to nowhere, downwind
but almost still and heads
down eating as if last

meals are being served,
clear air never gained,
then paws up to scrape
away particulate and
anguish, with audacity.

SHALLOW BREATHING

The heat takes the air out of your lungs
and won't let it back in; agitation is your
best hope to get any breath at all, to compile
a level of oxygen; there's no relaxing into
new eras or sinking into a past that was
always restless, tense, troubled; allergies
are refractions of tissue; the day cools,
though not enough to draw a full breath
and break the pattern, the habit of *going out*
into the world, rite of passage blocked —
an obstruction or liability in the unsteady
atmosphere — moist dry moist dry dry
dry; see the insect perched on your hand
work its trachea to the core of its being
as you breathe rapidly and with less effect —
a crusader beetle which is out of its
usual time of flourishing, it stays on
your hand and it might be developing
lungs, changing the very nature of its
body fluids while its cross changes
to an asterisk, a mark of complex
breathing as holy or unholy as the flight
which it's preparing for, though holding
back from releasing its stink because
it's just not anxious and is comfortably
reconfiguring the data you have to go by...
and there's nothing martial about its flight...

not crusading nor vectoring or westernisation...
fully body breath tubed as you exhale inevitability;
all those essences of breath you don't have but believe in,
all the parts of being you can't find or may have lost,
worn down since birth and your first cry; shallow
breathing seems a lament for all forms of verse
that will escape and never make their way in,
and you fear you are being disrespectful,
though control is the way through
to shadow as much as body, as plants
know at night; you might lapse into REM
sleep as breath struggles, *aut viam*,
superspreader of the vacuum.

THE PENGUIN CASTLE (PERTH ZOO CIRCA 60s AND 70s)

Horror fantasy ice castle in heatwave
fairy penguin kingdom, as said in my earlier
poem, 'Zoo Visits', the launch of access,
the performance to consolidate paternal memory,

    imprint, as now in illness my son
    watches on a separate screen
    as I watch on this one, emperor
    penguins raising chicks in Antarctic

winter snowstorms, on plains
and amidst ice crenellations
but no conquest and usurping,
rather a bringing into memory

    though now a freezing is less freezing
    and ice lessening over the ocean.
    In the food-stifled moat the penguins
    flurried, lost to the conditions

and replaced by slick otters,
though they lost their way too.
Such are lines of paternity, recalled
to the flock in inclement conditions

with their own harsh beauty
which a penguin castle in a zoo
can never ever have. Haunted
by the goodwill of visits now

my father is gone —
out of his element.

KANGAROO COURT

We had a pet kangaroo saved from the pouch
of its shot mother. It was raised on a teat and mixture,

wrapped in baby blankets. Strangers would say
that its 'baby photos' were adorable. Those are

my arms around the bundle... and those are my brother's,
and those there are our mother's. When able

to leave this false pouch, it hopped cautiously
around the backyard, pawing the sky, gently

grazing on sharpish buffalo grass.
Following us around, trembling

in twilight. We played hand games.
It was a female, and we discovered the warmth

of her pouch, which made us recoil — this seemed
too private to know. She sometimes distrusted the dog,

a cocker spaniel, but at other times they relaxed
close to each other. When we moved up the coast,

she went to a wildlife sanctuary. Though I'd like
to think we visited, I can't remember. She lived with us

for a long time. We'd tried to give her a local name,
but got that wrong. Lifting on her tail to say something,

we interpreted differently. She never seemed
aggressive. Under her nostrils the lip parted and big teeth

gnawed the hay we offered — brought down
from the farm. The fences were too high

for her to clear. She preferred spending nights out,
and eventually stopped coming onto the back

verandah. So deeply implicated in our timelines,
I try now to turn it into a movie. There are

photos and they don't fade fast enough. Other
kids wanted to see her, but she kept a low profile.

Her middle toes left decisive marks in the sand.
She likely had children. Her eyes were so round.

BROWN JELLYFISH

The this is not a footnote to the bell shape
and heartbeat thump of jellyfish propulsion,
        but part of the rhythm of the poem. The
scattering of brown jellyfish by Jet Ski
and speed-boat is not part of this poem's
rhythm. The stranding on thin beaches
        where paperbark trees have been reduced
        to a single band, barely a conversation —
blisters under the bark, shreds of tenacity —
upsetting the rhythm. This is the trauma
of settler metrics, and why I harp on
        about the grounds for distress. That river
        I knew inside-out but didn't, washing
away inland visits, tasting the ag runoff
from an upstream I dreamt about, harvesting
insights, storing up observations: ringneck
        parrot to swans, galahs to stilts; but brown
        jellyfish where the sea's white spot salinity
reached perfectly, struggling with the land's saltiness
washed down from eroded bare paddocks,
from where the water was meant
        to be fresh. Substitutions bring energy
        and interest to a metrics, but it's all
fabrication. Swimming cautiously through
a bloom — limina of medusas — that wash
of a collective, embracing the suspension of silt

and dinoflagellate algae, solute
searching for solute, subaerials
and collectors, parsing dying suns on thinner
beaches washed by speed-boat wavelets.

SOUTHERN SHOVEL NOSE RAY REFLECTED ME

Because we are over 860kms from the sea,
sea-life is seeking us out. And this from
        the Southern Ocean, fifty years ago.
        A southern shovelnose ray flapping
the sand, excavating a makeshift lair.
        The sand inflects its mottled skin
        which refracts an inner self
I don't even know I possess.

My sense of direction was created
by rivers and paddocks, farm dams
        and jetties. But the shovelnose ray
        (in being southern) pointed out
an alternative direction. I couldn't touch
        the sand, and my lines weren't
        marked in feet. Stress was seaweed,
imprecision — instances of revelation.

It is shocking to see a passing crustacean
whipped out of contention. I decided
        to abandon stats. This far inland
        where sea is contrary, I look for fossils
in the air and see them. Terrifying.
        A southern shovelnose ray is argued
        to be a bit of shark, a bit of ray,
and reflects the ambivalence of memoir.

SQUID UNDER LIGHTS THAT BURN UP THE PLANET

The squid jiggers gather under the late-night jetty lightburn

try not to mourn through biological facts gleaned from reading

          but remember the bloody ink stains on the planks

those acts of turning inside out, the gravitationally welling eyes

                    glazed over loss of medium

and tentacles that caught sleek night's bycatch

                    torn into bait or bucketed.

'SAINT FRANCIS AND THE BIRDS': STANLEY SPENCER (1935)

I spent a long time talking with birds,
which didn't make any difference
to the anomalies we were dealing
with — less than mirages,
something similar to falling trees.

There was a Muscovy duck
I called Donna. She
had been a farmyard duck
but didn't lay eggs and was a loner.
I cradled her for hours and sang to her.

It was a soothing relationship
for both of us. There were other
'domesticated' birds around, and they
ate snails and talked among themselves.
They filtered water through their beaks

along the edges of the anomalies.
I mistakenly called them angels.
When I walked, I walked like Donna.
I wasn't imitating her. She walked like me.
I used my hands to illustrate a scene

but her left wing had been clipped
and she tilted into the lawn.
When the family went north,
she was released into the 'wild'.
She shouldn't have been,

though she quickly merged
with the flock of various species
that gathered at Blue Gum Swamp.
I'm not sure what she passed on
from our songwriting sessions.

I thought I had a vocation
and spoke to stained glass
which remained silent.
The rest of the family
knew I had many interests.

I grew older translating
the songs of birds
into the spaces
between lines of poems.
I refused to pick flowers

but handed out
bouquets of description.
Sometimes I didn't eat for days.
I didn't sleep. My clothes
disintegrated.

But always the birds
around 'caricatures' of location.
An inner-city parrot.
A muscovy mirage.
A warped opinion of myself.

GELORUP RINGTAIL POSSUM SPEAKS AGAINST RING ROAD AND DESTRUCTION OF ITS HOME

I am sure among the piles of woodchips
you'll speak of geometry and soil density,
of runoff and traffic flow, I am sure
you'll eye up what you've haven't yet
taken of the forest and speak of *people*
and *industry*, speak *development*
and *traffic flow*. Ringtails/ring roads
are interchangeable? You might even say
congestion and connectivity, and I am
sure the word 'relief' will come in there
somewhere. I am sure you can't or won't
believe that possums speak, or if you
are willing to accept we speak among
ourselves, then likely you won't realise
that we translate all you say within earshot.
And even if you understand that we
understand every word of destruction
you utter, you'd likely blame us
for not acting to protect each other.
Try speaking against a machine
coming down on you, or knocking
your head off. Brutal, isn't it? You humans
don't fare too well against machines either.
You've a history of treating people
like you treat the forest. A history
of abusing all life that knows the forest

as home. There's not many of us left,
we ringtails among the cockatoos
and myriad other 'species' you don't
bother acknowledging. And the great trees
of great span and welcome, even
the dead ones which live through
our occupancy, share knowledge
of languages you can't add
to your databases, to your pocket
translators. It would shock you
to hear what was said about you
and your activities, what we
say of you before you kill us.
Murder has many degrees,
doesn't it? Not for us. Not by you.

DINGOES HOWLING AROUND NULLARBOR ROADHOUSE AT NIGHT, 2010

Phenomenal range of vocalisations.
        Conversation, recitals, monodies;
chasing down the low-slung desiccated moon
to grab it by the hindquarters. Confronting. I can't
help that the sounds lure me out onto the plain.
        I stumble into a rabbit hole in the karst. I hear
        French *bof!* in my sleep. French-
        speakers talk about dingoes
moaning. I hear howling. I remember the dogs
no one wanted because they were 'part dingo'.
Detractors point out their 'crazed expression... mouth... eyes...
        gait'. Bigots. Dingoes close in on the roadhouse.
        We have arrived from Norseman after passing
        Madura near where the oldest dingo bones
were found in a cave. Someone is blaming mainland
thylacine extinction on dingoes. That's a distinct *bark*, whatever
is said about duration. Bark vs. bite. Someone is trying
        to feed a stressed dingo the remnants
        of their dinner, which the sign calls
a DEATH SENTENCE because it confuses the boundaries
between wildness and domestication — that only
the dingo will suffer. Seems likely. I am stumbling
        around blue bush trying to elevate, to float
on the phenomenal range of vocalisations.

OBBLIGATO: SERENDIPITY

Two young dogs are loose and running around the house,
down the tiers and up the banks, circling rainwater tanks,
        pissing on flywire doors and wall planks. For dogs
        to be running 'loose' in this district is a death sentence,
so, I ring the ranger. He arrives quicker than seems feasible
and gathers them to him. They love the interaction and lower
        their heads. I hold them as he clips leashes to their collars,
        and as we rub their backs he says, 'It's lucky they ended up
on this place — if they'd run onto many properties around here
they'd be shot on sight.' Dead. On site. I know that too, and he shakes
        my hand assuring me they'll find their way home,
        and that he'll let their 'owner' know it can't happen again.
I said I had worried that ringing was 'dobbing them in'.
No choice. There's only one other way it could end.
        So I am feeling elated in long prosaic lines of flow
        about two dogs so attached to each other they follow
each other's lead, wanting through doors and windows,
to track scents through the valley, when I come across
        fresh possum scats and trace them back to a York gum
        above the house, one with a hollow which no birds
seem to ever use for nesting and which we have watched
for years. Detecting scratch marks, I know the possum
        must have squeezed into the hollow and encourage
        my eyes to discern fur from bark and dead wood
to reveal a subtle then pulsating movement of fur, an uncanny
reworking of the sublime, and my lines of observance

        and revelry get shorter, more pared
        back into leaf tips and ideas of predawn
and dusk, eliding moments of certainty from doubt —
the dry high sun stirring dreams or nightmares,
        a disturbance in digestion
        brought on by the presence
of dogs and humans. How familiar can I be after
a year away? Likely not forgotten, but written out
        and now barely figured back in.
        I whisper up to the filled hollow,
the lines will get longer and longer, and the dogs
returned home where they will remember.

BARKING OWL DOUBTS LIFT

Barking owl doubts lift
as slogan of silhouette,
          each wingweight
          gives purchase against
bourgeois values of light on
the DOG EXERCISE AREA sign
          to unleash
          as frolic
between apartments
and river wall, jetty light
          immersion to parallel
          drought breaker
runoff from over the Scarp
into the cauldron of river, white-
          spotted jellyfish
          chiasmus fluctuating,
pulsing signs to read as sight permits.
Hunched barking owl unflares
          darkness out on a limb,
          ink wash foliage
to balance *lift* and *settle*,
floater of predatorial emphasis
          on river ecology,
          so whittled down
to the osteoporotic bones of smaller
and smaller creatures, even

miniscule wild dogs
running unseen
by the catchers, leaving pellets
as markers, falling from calligraphy
and those angles
of seeing into seeing,
ground-to-tree, reflection off non-
reflecting surfaces, *fly* but not *flee*
this statement
this diatribe
this slogan of barking out
warnings and pleas...
pleas and warning*s*.

ECHIDNA TREMENS

If you allow me, I will publish this account
of our meeting. It will include no description

of you, no 'observations', and will never
be as useful as field notes. No research will

reference my findings, because there will
be no findings. The wave-motion shakiness,

sensors constantly responding to changes
in terrain, are more about me unwittingly

sticking my nose into hallowed spaces
where it isn't wanted. But I took no photo,

sketched no likeness, painted no abstraction
that feeds on our interaction in any way

whatsoever. Just this text, written
with the shaky hand of surprise.

SCALES

Surprisingly harsh sound of passage — sandblaster,
stone grinder, percussionist; quickly on my distraction;

no gentle swish, no frisson with a slippery earth;

abrasive rustle, callous susurration, allegro vivace, heavy-duty
male in search of futurity, dugite to dugite compulsion;

no gentle swish, no smoothness with slippery earth;

head raised in functional emphasis of serpentine locomotion,
tongue flicker sensorium, scales modulating to shift states, terrain;

no gentle swish, no frisson with a slippery earth;

mating season, overwriting mouse burrows, close to my bared foot
but finding way of least impediment through to potential mate;

no gentle swish, no smoothness with slippery earth;

I am to be avoided and wish to avoid it, surprised;
I remember my elegy which spoke of the soul;

no gentle swish, no frisson with a slippery earth;

my diminished eyes will pick up a signature
where warmth was extracted from red bricks;

no gentle swish, no smoothness with slippery earth;

a confidence, a toner of toxin to print my exclamation
though I keep walking the same route, immediately after.

ONE HUMP OR TWO

A boutique farmer might joke: 'How do you like your camels,
        one hump or two?' We have both sorts out here
among the usual livestock and kangaroos. I could respond
        with the story of my great grandfather lost in the desert
being saved by a camel and cameleer, that I wouldn't even be here
        if it weren't for camels, which seems a tangentially
appropriate subtext to colonial farming. But I won't —
        this story would simply leave the camels stranded, pseudo-
ruminating. Necks arched over barbed wire, reaching
        for what might happen across another timeline,
in an alternative geography. These camels exist.
        They are being farmed where trees have been stripped
down to salinity. I've witnessed an emu studying a camel
        and vice versa, but not here. Both heads on long necks
working through the politics of global traversals, legacies.
Horses watch *these* camels, staring mainly at their toes.

SINGLED OUT

The sheep raised from a bottle and put back with the mob
gallops over to the fence and bleats. It has been granted *a name.*
It responds to *its name.* Many sheep have been hand-reared
        on farms and 'returned' to the demi-wild of paddocks.
        This named sheep has been castrated and placed with a mob of ewes.
It studies the visitor (fascinated by *its* behaviour) with eyes the visitor
considers 'uncanny', out of the ordinary, disturbing and unsettling.
Projecting, the visitors conjecture this sheep knows something it shouldn't.
        A visitor gets a frisson suggesting a risk. Something mythopoetic.
        The person who was responsible for feeding and raising
this sheep — little teat-puller as a lamb, a nuzzler and bumper,
a real card and a character — is amused and delighted
by the visitor's reactions, and says, 'Don't worry, this one
        will die a natural death or simply of old age. Eventually,
        it will forget us and never respond, and its eyes will become
much the same as other sheep eyes. But out of nostalgia
and that disquiet that we don't want to pass on to next
generations, we will let it live, unless we sell the farm.'

HYMN OF THE SQUIRRELS

Not an issue of 'variety', of red, brown, grey and black,
but of presence. Not an issue of contact,
but of fruits and storage. Tree-rise and leap:
collect, nibble, compile. Each catoptric joy.

Terror is never far away: the cyclist
with squirrel skins hanging from handlebars,
the percussion of small arms fire among
the blasts of deer hunters and pig shooters.

A hymn is not only praise, it's a tangent of status quo.
As part of squirrel-world, we survey ratios
of refuge and shelter in zones of foray. I never
think of Pascal when 'lost' in a forest, only after.

Almost secular in a religious country, the leaves are lost
and squirrels become more visible, then not.

EXIT/ENTRY

Mud dauber wasps
are eating their way
out of nesting chambers.

They will leave their
grub-life of darkness,
hungering

after an idea
of light. And they
crave nectar,

not the decomposed
matter of spiders
they didn't know

were 'spiders',
not yet. They are
eating out into light

you can hear them
from inside
the house

where your heart
beats too fast
and you shelter

from sunlight
which is far
too sharp.

PIE-DISH BEETLE PURSUES LONGER LIFE

I know of only one pie-dish beetle
actively pursuing a longer life
   but there may have been
   and probably are still others
determinedly engaged in the same
undertaking. Approaching the end
   of its year on earth,
   turning its flange
to edge off predators, combing
night ground for decaying
   vegetable matter,
   it considers its diet
and becomes more particular.
How decayed, what species of plant,
   how rapidly consumed,
   which morsels might prove
restorative, how much time should be
dedicated to resting and dreaming?
   Further, it is constantly
   working on memories
of close calls and dubious encounters,
learning which insects to avoid,
   how to stay away
   from nightbirds
and foxes under a burning moon.
With no flight possible, it knows
   the ground with an intensity

turned to advantage:
rocks live so much longer and are to be
envied and possibly imitated.
Adapting instinctual
responses and inherited
recall, sharing experiences
with other pie-dishes,
even if self-obsessed.
In the extreme dry
taking summer into winter, flange
collecting the scant dew, converting
it into persistence
and unsentimental
imagery. Pragmatic, determined, visionary.
Tinged blue and searching out blue zones
across the valley-side,
through the public
reserve. Not interested in patents and profit,
this beetle is sure that once its life
goes beyond
the known limit
it will see some point in 'letting go.'
I'm not counting the days.

THE STING OF A EUROPEAN WASP

The chemistry is so easily poetic;
doing the language work and adding
tangents to metaphors. We might

almost get lost in it, unless
we're composing shortly
after the sting has set in.

With me, this is almost a trope.
Self-parody. But a different
sting and a different poison.

Antihistamine, ice on the swelling.
The wasp long flown and able
to sting again and again,

as needs be. This goes with
living in an attic with roof
windows — looking up

into the sky as you coax
the wasp back out, dazzled
by everything that's happening.

BED SCORPION

A bed scorpion
    skirrs across
nameless flowers
in counterpane diamonds —
    tail hooked, acute
    tear-shaped sting poised.
It flattens, still,
    tail twist-folded
    alongside, then
up and rapid again
to plunge over
    the rippled foot
    and vanish.
I don't know how
it behaved overnight,
    how long it was
    with us. Between
mattress and bed base,
in the folds, hoping
    for what we
    might draw
to us — hot on a hot night,
restless as conditions.

SHOVELER DUCK

The shoveler
digs a hole
in water

but once down
it wants out
with more

than it went in
with — matter
created —

& the walls
of the hole
collapse

as fast
as the shoveler
shovels:

cascade.

NOT ON FRIDA KAHLO'S *WOUNDED DEER*, NOT REALLY?

When the bow hunters sported deer from the woods near Gambier
I was not thinking of Frida Kahlo's *Wounded Deer*, which I do now.
This is not appropriate in many ways, but maybe it is in others.

When the pickup truck with the stag in the back secured so the antlers
were *safe* — wall trophy, obviously — but the hindquarters flopping
and bouncing on the open tailgate, hooves kicking off the road's asphalt

(and I imagine sparks but it was flecks of staling blood) roared
past me on the road through the village, I was not thinking of Frida
Kahlo's *Wounded Deer*, which I do now. Maybe I should have then?

But now I am thinking it through, in another hemisphere, over
 fifteen years
later. I am trying to be the deer and the stag but not be Frida Kahlo —
I would never try to do that. Which makes me wonder as I unloose

arrows out from my skin — nine times I quiver, nine times I transfer
my essence to a tree, nine times I shape the memory into something
 visceral —
am I really seeing the past *now*? There are no deer here, but there are

kangaroos and they suffer similar fates. I cannot see Frida Kahlo's
head on a kangaroo, I cannot build the symbolism, archetypes and set
of personal references. I won't mystify. If the sea at the end of a
 wooded path

is forced into the sky, so too are the hills of the valley into a different
but intimately connected sky. Wrong images. I wonder about
translations of *karma*,
and reach for my feet to see if they are secure on an earth that turns fast

or maybe it's just turning at the necessary speed. Neither fast nor slow.
Maybe
that speed will stay the same no matter what the miners, industrialists
and adventurers
do to speed in all our names. It frightens me (and honestly, I don't
frighten easily —

well, not in a personal sense, anyway) that I have nothing to do with
Frida
Kahlo or her deer stag or her injury or bare forest or fetish for arrays
of nine.
But then, why would I use a word like 'fetish'? What am I painting
here?

RESIDUES: SHE-WOLF, LEOPARD, LION

NO ANIMALS WERE HARMED IN MAKING THIS LOOK
sings the Instagram vanguard for the Schiaparelli couture show
at Paris Fashion week, people astonished at how *lifelike*

the head of a lion, the leopard out of the breast, the she-wolf
shouldered by a super model. Super. Model. Animal rights
groups protest the fetishisation, another defending 'the look'

as 'anti-trophy'. *Everyone* is talking about Dante again, even
though his 700th death celebrations have well and truly wrapped up.
I don't visit zoos but was taken to them as a child. I saw

the lion, the wolf and the leopard. Well, I saw a lion, leopard
and a dingo, which the zoo describes as a DOG-LIKE WOLF.
There were male and female dingos. There were she-dingoes.

I couldn't find my way to God, but a light in a window
suggested I might. I thought, One day I will illustrate Dante's
Inferno, though I had no idea what it was truly about.

My mother said that she, her parents and sister could hear
the lions at the zoo roaring four and a half miles away.
The leopards were silent. The dingoes bothered their

consciences. For me, the odour of restraint hasn't diluted.
NO ANIMALS WERE HARMED IN MAKING THIS LOOK
Setting off on my journey, I thought there was enough of me

to feed the world's wickedness. I wanted to return the animals
to their natural environments. It wasn't complicated. Not for me —
I couldn't believe they were real in those cages. But then,

nothing seemed 'life-like'. This sense of things didn't inure me
to their suffering, but complicated my relationship to literature
and art. I don't visit zoos, but went to one with a fellow activist

during the late '90s. I met Dante, Blake and ergonomics.
The documentation of witness was lost to figurative language.
I regret the early similes and metaphors of earlier encounters.

Lion, leopard, she-wolf. The heave and sway of empires.
NO ANIMALS WERE HARMED IN MAKING THIS LOOK
Vandals have been defacing the Colosseum. Again. Ipso facto.

CHINESE WATER DEER

Across the path, through the hedge, down
a private road. Property is not her obsession.

Feeding on a dry summer's day in Cambridge,
near the Isaac Newton Institute for Mathematical Sciences,

she nibbles in spirals, and I follow the rhythm
which won't be augmented. The forecast

is for a rainy night, so she'll swim
the roads, countermanding the draining

of the fens. Alone, like me, but I'm
meeting a friend to walk by the Granta,

where we might watch a squirrel eat haws
in a hawthorn tree, and a grey heron

turn away, refusing better sides.
And those inlets in the riverbank —

regular and wavering, possible
entry points for when the deer

wants to find her way down to the sea.
She has tusks. She is prepared.

BROWN LONG-EARED BAT (MID-SUMMER)

I'd just read three poems about bats
among dozens of poems about animals.
Those poems did not name the types
of bats, but generalised. The bat

experience was a human experience,
an extension of something else going
on in lives, or a *useful* (if surprised!)
tool to make some personal point.

Walking from the library to the flat,
past thickened evergreens, I saw the bat
pitchpole into another mode of reception.
It had shut down echolocation.

It had denied its description:
physical and behavioural.
It was dealing with a political
and ethical issue. It fell, then lifted.

BACK AT COLLEGE AFTER TWO AND A HALF YEARS AWAY, I AM 'STUDIED' BY THE GREY HERON STANDING IN THE SAME PLACE IN THE SAME WAY

I am testing the boundaries of history
and have observed that it's much less

about humans than is presumed.
Each sampling of animals *as animals*,

of poems 'about' animals, exposes
an overemphasis on *humans*. It's not

a matter of those old deceptions — pathetic
fallacy and anthropomorphism

(animals *wish* for some equality!) —
but *the case itself*: everything serving

a human interest. There are no
poems written by animals available

to me, though I try to keep my senses
open. The grey heron standing

in the same place and in the same way
two and a half years from when I last saw it

might be either playing a game
or enacting the deeply familiar

or both — one eye searching beyond
reflections and lily pads. Read:

average life span is 'five years in the wild'
and up to' twenty-three years has been recorded'.

They have been collated. *Cohabitating*
with humans. Tolerating humans.

Appalled by mimicry in sculptures and text,
or expecting me to appear just as I was when I left,

to compare anatomies in the same manner,
against the same topography, two and a half years

further on in a history it has paralleled
or intersected or denies.

SLOW WORM

The steep path
        down to Bebenhausen
                sunning in the shade
                        drawing warmth
                of rising day
        thigmothermic utterance
but vulnerable
        to joggers'
                thundering
                        downward motion.
                I encourage to leave
        the path for its safety
a touch of the tail
        thrice and incrementally
                into the grass and leaves
                        edging to live longer
                years into decades
        we count as witness
when we also endure.

CRUELTY

Reports say that someone
        around the Tübingen region
                has been torturing
and killing slow worms.

These superb creatures
        appear on pathways
                absorbing the sunlight;
        we might encourage
them to slip into the grass
to prevent a cyclist or car
        riding over them,
        hellbent
on their destination.

That anyone
        would tear them to bits,
                would empty the sun
                from inside them
        is beyond
conception.

But people do this
        to other people.
People make entertainment
        out of such acts.

Cruelty is meted out
    by institutions
    and imitated
by the lost and damaged.

Reports say that someone
    around the Tübingen region
        has been torturing
and killing slow worms.

FIRE SALAMANDER

The fire salamander
killed by a vehicle
on the forest path, will
not be there
when we next walk
to Bebenhausen.

You might think
it had given
up its body, splayed
over the cinders,
but it hadn't
and never will.

The buzzard
with branch-width wings
falls in to assist
with transference,
but is refused.

The small suns
fluctuating
in salamander skin
showed us a way past.

We didn't
take its image
with us. Not
even here.

MARSH FROG CALLS TO THOSE CROUCHING IN HOLES

Yes, give us a chance,
pulling ourselves out of holes
and leaping through moss
architraves into *der Teich*!

A croak-quack like a duck in flight —
and a big bold duck at that —
ventriloquist, reverberating
all over the show, and vocal sacs

blowing transparent to deflate
as marks of a short attention span.
Fascinating, for sure, but it's as
if we're at your beck and call.

Frantic around the lily pads,
worried about *who's* where
in relation to *you* — but the sun
is rising higher, and sadness

will fall on us all. Big with bluster,
mustering us — the nerve! Loud as a duck.
And though we can't help but join a chorus,
we must think of our own quack acoustics.

CLOUDS OF DARK-WINGED FUNGUS GNATS [DEMI-TANKA]

i.

Dark-winged fungus gnats
engulf me, and one is trapped
behind glasses I'll
remove, gently blowing it
back into the waiting cloud.

ii.

Firebugs below
the cloud continue across
the laneway — heat draws
enough moisture to suspend
all our doubt, enhance the day.

iii. inverted

I enter the cloud hoping
to emanate at some point,
but, deep inside this
meteor shower, wonder
what shape I'll be in.

iv.

Close mouth, hold breath, tap
those old underwater skills.
Think positive, don't
flail arms around and upset
the Brownian assumptions.

v.

Visualising this
habitat, take on gnat-brain-
eye coordinates:
shade before leaves have emerged;
obstacles sudden, like me.

CADMUS AND HARMONIA

Blue-tongued skink is what I will be
though I don't expect you to join me.
Just let me live in your vicinity, eating
capeweed flowers and the odd tomato.

My mother sent a picture of a blue-tongue
that has likely lived around her for years —
it wakes into awakening, sunning
in the overheating with its solar panels

taking in too much heat too early.
It's not true it they we can never
get enough. That's a message
from home. I don't expect

you to join me, but please
understand that such a shift
is inevitable. It started in childhood,
when I kept a dead snake in methylated

spirits, turning it to the light
to detect life after death. And it clarified
as my brother rescued skinks from roads,
and I left the snake sad in a dark shed

and joined him in harsh sunlight,
my blue tongue out, wondering how much
more heat a cold-blooded animal can take,
how soon before we must bask in the shade.

VOCATIVE

Cat is the opening of cataclysm and cathartic
but it has nothing to do with prefixes

or roots, which cats don't eat. The key is catalyst
while admiring their spirit and intelligence

and lamenting annihilations in bushland or neighbourhood,
especially on those frilly edges and around hedges

where birds and reptiles trip a cat's senses.
How a word ends is also a delusion —

the magnificat sings requiescat — garland
of feathers, coat of scales, though we love

them to remind us of ourselves;
sleek as a catchphrase: inculcating.

DOGS

Actaeon — deer man — the dogs
are at your heels; you trained

them to pull you to the ground,
to rip into flesh. Even with coats,

your dogs are naked. That's
what sets you apart — the desire

to cover yourself, to uncover
others. The huntress hides

behind her clothes of blood,
washed away in the pool, naked.

It's furious guilt that drives
her vengeance. You can name

every dog. In a single walk
to and through the forest

you'll see terriers and rottweilers,
spaniels and shepherds,

retrievers, bulldogs, dachshunds,
greyhounds and pointers.

The relationship of dogs
to their 'owners'. Actaeon,

deer man, last thoughts
of bewilderment and fear.

HORSE NOISES

Just because I blow my lips like a horse
doesn't mean I am becoming a horse,
        not entirely a horse
        anyway; I love horses,
but don't know precisely when horse
noises became emphatic in my horse
        vocabulary; horse
        teeth grinding down horse
hooves wearing on troubled horse
ground; that's me, expressive horse
        nickering, never horse
        neighing, never horse
whinnying, and though a distinctive horse
change has come about, I don't notice horse
        until it's drawn to my horsey
        attention; I say, at least horses
are vegans, and rumination is horse
contemplation in the light of horse
        nebulae, where horse
        stars are born making horse
noises, blowing through stellar horse
lips to signify resignation, a love of horses.

PEGASUS

Each day striking the stony path
through the forest of deer ticks —

watched by nine sad magpies
that had been human —

Pegasus is led by the woman
who talks of a greener past,

who knew the magpies
before they were trapped

in this myth of origin.
The things they repeat!

Each day striking the stony path,
waiting for fresh springs

that never get started, wings
tucked tight as forgetting.

ORPHEUS

Playing by ear
each version of me

suits an agenda.
I make use of paths

made by animals,
get my bearings

via sunspots, starfall
and the flight

of birds. So many
trees are people

but so few people
were trees. A shortfall.

Flowers are string
instruments.

EURYDICE

The music of *gasp!*
of surprise —

snake memory
is vein-work.

I have always
expected the back-

over-the-shoulder
glance — a look

of doubt rather
than longing.

Here, the asp viper,
back there, the dugite.

Academics want access
to rockstars, making me

expendable. The music
of inevitable surprise.

CALLISTO

Wiping out the bears
of Western Europe

and desiring
a slice of outer space —

through the roof windows
I see enough stars

to make a plough —
the European Space Agency

has its colonial
launch place.

If the stars are still alive,
the corn crop will rise

and fall with the hunter's call —
a gunsmith's astrology.

EUROPA

I have avoided walking through the settlement and barn area of the
'open' farm
on the edge of town. I always branch away or head down towards the forest.
But I *have* recorded the electric fences and shooting towers, the dark barns
and the shit encrusted cows allowed to graze (rarely) in apple-treed
meadows.
I have seen horses from a nearby 'riding school' being ridden and walked,
segueing farm and forest. I have juxtaposed the power plant that focalises
the liminal between apartments and fields. All of that, and a cross-section
of other edges. But today I walked through the centre of production and
read
the BIO signs of milk and slaughter, and saw the heavily uddered cows
in their stalls, and the barns full of the hay and silage, the high-protein feed
brought in from shimmering crops. A reality brutal as warfare, but
reassuring
for the consumers who want to be close to the source. A hawk wing painted
on a banner swings in a barn entry. Calves, kept in agonising proximity
to their mothers, feed on shadows. There are plenty of poems detailing
the agonising wrongs of this agriculture. Some allude to rape and sexual
abuse,
which this industry is built around. One cow I have seen outdoors, quickly
eating sunshine, tells me it has been nicknamed 'Europa' (in all languages),
continuing: 'The sheds are islands. The sea changes like crops and fallowness
under a three-field system. We are *bio*! I must speak quickly because I'll
be back
indoors in an hour or so. I am to be prepped for insemination. *See*, the crows
are nesting! Or have nested. Apples fall or have fallen. We are so locked
into *your* sense of time that we are time-invariant. Have you ever written

about gender and meat as opposed to gender and milk? Seduction and rape
are *so close* in Greek mythology, or so I've heard farmers and consumers
intimate.
We are rhetorical devices. We are forced into many modes of nearness,
of *touch*.
And then when we actually desire touch it is stopped — the nuzzled calf
is hidden
in the dark. There's not much discussion of love in the market, though
human lovers
walk past us regularly. Through the cracks in the barns I have caught sight
then turned away, embarrassed. They will eat us to fuel their complexities.'
Translating this is an imperfect science, but as most chroniclers say
to their patrons and masters: 'I offer this flawed document humbly
and hope it serves.' I won't walk that way again, but I will pass close
and this limits my skill and my vocabulary.

INNER RHINO FREES ITSELF FROM THE *PANZERNASHORN*

They are sure they can keep it locked down
as street sentinel, driving off enemies

and luring customers, statement of strength
and mascot credentials — yes, stomping

paradoxes outside Zürcher Kantonalbank's HQ
along the Bahnhofstrasse, close to the outfall

of the lake into the Limmat, quickish flowing
but tepid with the melt of secret accounts,

preventing it from charging into cradled water,
dousing all that pent-up cold sweat rage

which they have tapped: endangered species,
horn of plenty, battlefield juggernaut,

warning stance as offensive disposition
of a weaponised investment. It would

be too brutal, too insensitive to put it sharply:
mimicry of a kill zone; reflectionless mirror-plating.

Deceptive yearning accusing withdrawn
piercing anguished aporic eyes.

Could it be said to yearn those years in the zoo
while HQ was renovated? Will it survive

the covert and the obvious? Will it remain
many things to many people? Is rust

a blood-borne disease or a blessing in disguise?
Be sure it thinks about the strength of swans,

their armour against stories told about them
they can't relate to, their demi-graceful slow-lift flight.

MAX PLANCK

As the Institute
for Intelligent Systems
builds itself slab by slab,
it wonders which euphemisms

will grab the workforce's
interest, recommending
some 'green features'
for a commodious future.

Sure, the institute will want
time off, worried that blackbirds
and blue tits aren't being
hyphenated by its sensors.

PROTEST

European green woodpecker
foraging among blue metal stones

in a car park that will soon fill
with the official end of summer.

Up suddenly to apex of pine tree,
head tilted back, calling out in calque,

making a point, working a mode
of protest the campaigners won't know.

MIDDLE SPOTTED WOODPECKER

The woodpecker following
you, or at least going the route
tree by tree over the path,
is not evidence of neurodiversity.

But the woodpecker doing
precisely the same thing tomorrow —
flight-tap-tap-flight-tap-tap-flight —
might suggest the possibility.

AVIARIES

If we could fly further than largesse,
further than a faux expanse,
        beyond the game trees,
we might change forms. We are no more
fixed than seed bells and cuttlebones,
        no less able to create synonyms
or suffer the attributions of homonyms.
We are the fate of light mixed with anatomies.
        And yet, you'd have us perceive
an external world through a grid,
have us claw and beak the barriers,
        scale those outer limits. Monitoring,
controlling our environments, you rule
out sin, affirm your unified plexus.

ANIMALIA UTOPIA

Every creature ever. Every single one was there.
Every animal that ever existed. Everyone
who ever existed. All life of the animal kingdom
but without hierarchies. A kingdomless kingdom.

Not even the vaguest notion of kings or ladders.
Not a species-based filling in of the catalogue,
but rather each and every individual
in a state of co-existence: eternal bliss.

The eaters of others were between meals
and their meals existed as the animals
they were. All living, all at once. From the earliest
phases of abiogenesis, there was no evolution,

just mutual timeless *come as you are* existence.
Whether in jungles or forests or oceans or rivers
or roof eaves or carpets or stormy or clear skies,
whether at night or midday in hot deserts or ice ages.

All of it coexisting. So many languages overtalking
made for a beautiful and insistent hum that was so beyond
the senses you'd *reach for it* an architecture of living matter
harmonising in the moment without moral censure.

All in that living moment somewhere on its own timeline.
So many timelines paused and not a trace of 'survival of the fittest'.
And what was bizarre — really the only bizarre aspect —
was the secret manuscript by Ted Hughes

in which there was no tooth and claw,
no bloody realism of nature, but magnificent equity.
Even entropy and putrefaction were on hiatus
other than when they were part of the glorious

existence of themselves. Things were gratuitously lush!
The lines burgeoned with hyperbole but without a glimpse
of bathos. A maggot smiled, but what it had been consuming
was alive and well and eternal. I leapt

through the paradoxes. Hopped from oxymoron
to tautology, from superfluity to incongruity!
It all made perfect sense. They made perfect sense,
And I was enmeshed in it. Now, I *might* have dreamt

this all up (as the trope goes), but when I woke,
a camel walked through the eye of a needle,
and blue-banded bees flew from the florets
that had been my eyes. From my ears

swam dolphins and pythons,
my nose harboured bats and stick insects,
and from the vegetalia of my lips
spilled blank taxonomies.

THE ARTISTRY OF ZOOGRAPHIA

When the Western Australian Acclimatisation Committee
was established at the end of the nineteenth century,
it seems worth *remembering* that it was a dual-purpose body:

to summon 'familiar' species to the colony to make settler
life less uncanny, more reassuring, and also to establish
a zoological garden. When modern zookeepers

call out 'the committee' for its colonial self-interest,
and pat themselves on the back for *their* own commitment
to 'conservation' and the purity of scientific research

(zoos no longer mere precincts of entertainment),
the removal of animals from their native environments
and their transportation across the zones of the world

seem to slip between the planks and bars and glass-
walls through which visitors supposedly gain
a sense of the astonishing diversity of life.

Zoo visitors are part of the experiment, part of the solution.
The deletion of the palm squirrel which had acclimatised
to the surrounding suburbs (the greener wealthier

river-side enclaves), the transfer of kookaburras to dismantle ecosystems, and the dream of deer parks and well stocked sport-fishable rivers, are ingredients of an old zoography,

PRing into a sustainable future.

GOOSE GIRL AND GOOSE BOY FIGURINES

No story attached, I am told. Maybe
a wedding present to my grandparents,
and always favoured by my grandmother
in the living room glass-fronted cabinet —
etched glass of palms and birds
out of their comfort zones, mixed
ecologies, disparate tales and testimonies.

My mother has them now, that set,
though the goose boy's head is semi-
secured with Blu Tack. *Remembering*
is a flaw we rely on — the fabrics
expressed in porcelain, the eternal
gaze of the pair who never quite
look at each other no matter how you
position them.

I would have placed
them on different glass shelves
so they could make their own ways,
unhindered.

No, it's not the romance
of the boy and the girl, not the shared
plight of a brother and sister and their
labour in the farmyard, rather it
was and is *the geese*, three on each

plinth, two reaching towards the cloth sling
of feed opening up, one beak to the earth
picking what has already spilled,
and then stretching further down
into chasms of perdition. I feared
they might be French geese destined
to be fattened till they pop, while
the children starved, but the costumes
seemed wrong. Or geese to quilt
a colder Europe, soften the fall
into a warmer sleep. Past tense.

Where *were* they from? A factory in Germany
but 'Dutch'? 'Breton'-speaking? I had
no idea, and now can't track it down.
But the same factory, their fates linked.
Stamped with numbers, out of sight
unless you know where to look. How to interpret.

When the lights are out
and the mopoke speaks,
the geese remain silent. I know
because I have listened.

I could give them a story, but won't.
Not really, not completely.
These geese that won't fly,
these geese colouring ground

and sky, the tint of manufacture,
the mantels they will tend and nurture.

If the horse's head speaks
from the provincial dish, and the goose
refuses to be caught, and the girl
will keep her hair hidden
as the sweet-faced boy lusts
after someone else when we're
out of sight, what will collectors
say when the damage becomes clear,
the farmyard compromise revealed?

I hazard a guess: that in the touches
of blue and yellow and Rhone red wash —
faces drained, transfixed,
dutiful, goose, gander, geese —
there's a suppressed wildness.
Paired and trapped. Companion pieces.
Gaggled. And no stories attached.

REMNANT BUSHLAND ANTI-FANTASIA

Grim as an archipelago that wasn't there until so recently the astonishment of a sea that changed from brown to green to yellow to brown again shocking as a fantasia of occupation; innuendo of gaps in fences and over the range of bounce a delusion of replantings in plastic collars less astonishing to rabbits, scales on the grass tree and scratch of hakeas a stretching to bridge island to island clump to clump resonance of hollow to hollow; heat haze hemistich that alliterates heroic grain codes that don't fit don't subscribe ant trails and bared patches of underearth, a drift of concoction to silo a privileged redundancy; echidna flex to tip the boulder, to sign the outcrop, branch diagram of oils and bracts, uncapping of fibrils, glass-smash arterial tear as encircling traction engines auto-tune grunt and despair, qualities of leisurely observation, of artiness in the percentage parings; rather, reach stick to stick, processional caterpillar column to columnar method subtracting and subtracting as determined to correlate blue-banded bees burrowing in the sandier banks alongside seasonal rainbow bee-eater counterpoints, how could you pretermit?

Such worthy mythopoeia of replacement, of one hand then the next, pillar over dinner plate, plough disc of post after post strung concordantly. We join with chatter, we stick hands in 'til fingers splay and rhizome faux wisdoms, desperate to controvert? Scansion of fingernail seed, all that hard yakka, all that involvement and commitment, all that integrity harbouring marsupials: but seriously, but seriously we mean it. Just best steps conjured out of the scenic, out of the brutalised, out of the tangeticides of living a multifaceted life: oat cake and acacia seed cake, too. Pitching in as drought-resistant, inquiring after ancient knowledges, signposting respect. For sure. Absolutely. But withering after planting, withering when downpour cuts from paddock to remnant, and divagating for an evening's viewing of sunset, possessive as not, introspective as the buzz of protecting and 'discovery'. And magnetic resonance chopper mining drop zone implants, overfly to suss out rarities to assault and battery transport to glow a new lithium-plated future. Scraps of counterweight, but, nevertheless, less in those crosswinds.

BOTANICA ABSENTIA

This open house below the crest of hill
with some annexes glassed-in — each micro-
environment under the sway of local
specifications and larger globular forces.

It's not the same alone, bullfinch. And why
is a consistent register the barometer
of worth for a splinter or slab of words
we call 'verse'? Angle of sun is to arrays

of receptors as dog is to soil profile
in a manger of nationalist poets. And then,
muniment comforts of saunter rising
in the easy manner of suspicions, an

odour of old or ersatz pollen, catenary
borders and ductile barriers.

DRONE-MIMEO-AVIAN-SPOLIATION-SURVEILLANCE

> '... We've taken the land from them, we were cutting down roosting and nesting trees ... The airspace was the only place that was for the birds.'
> —Gisela Kaplan, *ABC News*

Drone-mimeo-avian-spoliation-surveillance,
        deciphering our bird desiring
we delete birds while taking their pictures,

which doesn't serve the requirements
        for ambiguity in the art we make
to fulfil ourselves or sell on the art market.

Drone-mimeo-avian-spoliation-surveillance
        is a honing of eye-hand co-ordination
like developing 'twitch' response

in violent video gaming. *Down below*
        sweeps by in such cascading
and free-flowing spans — a wing

span parody that lulls us into flight-
        dream scenarios, bird's eye view more
        than a bird's eye edited with resolution.
Drone-mimeo-avian-spoliation-surveillance.

PHILEMON AND BAUCIS

Bark grew over their mouths at different times —
my grandfather's last words coming years before
my grandmother's. She said she was looking forward
to joining him in the afterlife, and then the bark grew
over her mouth, too. They were gardeners. We often
ate meals at their house as kids, and then spent
time hiding in the garden, transforming, transpiring.

I was just speaking on the phone with my father's wife
of five decades about his situation — near death,
then a slight rally, though rallying to move away
again. He has *had enough.* Wants to move on alone.
For the first time in months, I hear his voice —
at the edge of the phone mic's range...
his foreground, the hospital bed that holds
his contortions, frustrations... picking up
the stretch of syllables till they make new language,
till they sound like a strong wind through
the dry leaves of the forest of his childhood. He
doesn't sound like a child. He sounds like himself,
but different. He sounds like a strong wind
in a forest of dry leaves anywhere in the world.
Though he cannot form words, his meaning is clear:
he wants to know who is on the other end of the phone.
I don't know if he thinks the gods have forsaken
him, but I doubt it. He doesn't seem to have ever
thought like that, though his wife does occasionally.

Here in Tübingen, lightning has been striking
buildings, trees and people. Storm-speech
is a desire to come into the home as a guest.
The storms expect to be worshipped.
Dad's wife is constantly with him.
She knows how to hear most sounds
he makes, their qualities of a new language.

As I eat the food Tracy has prepared,
I know the work that goes into love.
I cannot imagine living just to watch her
throw down roots into an underworld,
to grow taller than the sky into an overworld.
I want the bark to grow over my mouth first,
after I've said a farewell, and for it to cover
my eyes so I don't see her suffering.
I will grow leaves for memories,
which won't be stripped from me
by any changing seasons, any ending.
I will wait until she is the tree close to me
that will defy the paradox of a flooded
burning earth, that will bring fresh air
into the afterlife, into the habitat.

HÖLDERLINIANA

Air Kisses for Hölderlin's Avatar

Blowing air kisses as he looks
anywhere but at me. I think
        our relationship becomes more
        meaningful the less I remember
of his poetry in translation.
There's a leaf in his stony hair.

We're speaking a language
of gestures, trees, sparrows, indifference,
        proportions, and over-enthusiasm (all mine).
        I cast a different geography into his spectrum,
but this being a statue in a botanical garden
it causes less distress to his avatar.

Which doesn't make it right.
Just a fact, like measurements.
        I am not sure how precise
        I can manage to be. As Tracy says,
between dubbed Star Trek series
(I know every word in *American*)

and a collected Hölderlin Gedichte *only*
in German, I will *really* learn
        to speak or read *something*. I say
        Hallo and *Danke* to the classical

pose — to those far away eyes,
with these damned air kisses.

Apotheoses and the Hölderlin Monument, Old Botanical Gardens, Tübingen

My father is in his last hours
and I stand beside the statue I don't want
    to pull down, have my photo
    taken. To *take* a photo. Or its past
participle. I am thinking of students
who worship the poet,
    and I am thinking of the missing
    arm of this 'Hellenic' Hölderlin,
which I learn held a laurel
before it was damaged, stolen.
    'Vandalised'. This happened
    in the nineteenth as well as
twentieth century. All
that protrudes from the right
    shoulder is a tarnished metal pin.
    In Perth, my father has stopped
wanting to live. Last night he had another
stroke. He is in the private anguish
    of dying and wants it to remain private. Ergo,
    I wouldn't presume to talk about light,
and he wouldn't want to hear.
He never worshipped the old gods
    of Greece and never wanted
    to climb Mount Parnassus.
He was the top apprentice
mechanic in Western Australia

each year of his apprenticeship.
He went to a minuscule bush school.
He lived with his mum, dad and sister
at Gleneagle where each was the other's
lightning rod. Jarrah trees were monuments.
He wouldn't have vandalised a statue
even if it made no sense to him.
Personally, I don't care what happens
to a statue of an explorer
or aristocrat, but I see the statue
of such a poet differently. I am
comfortable having my photo
taken alongside it, mounted
in the old botanical gardens where trees
were sampled and cultivated from around
the world. The collectors have gone, many trees
remain. The oldest tree is native
to the region — a 250-year-old
beech tree. Its roots are uneasy.
It's not far from the God-like
statue of, or to, Hölderlin, who suffered
in his life and was no god.
He felt pain gods can't feel.
My father's body is breaking down.
And as he wants to leave life,
it's not his will that's broken —
in fact, I am sure that it's thriving,

like the reach of the statue's
    missing limb, the laurel already
    bestowed upon us,
whatever our failings,
whatever we've cherished.

Blasphemy

Hölderlin is the poet with a tower and a statue,
          but he's not the only poet of this town,
          by no means, historically or relatively.
There are uglier histories.
And his wasn't easy, and is a pit
          of Romanticism. All the points
          of repair, all the allusions. It
would be a kind of blasphemy
to deny his presence, his intensity.
          The leaves are falling differently
          this year. The only evidence
I have is intuition. The yellows
are off-yellow, the browns
          possibly less russet, the reds
          tending towards orange.
I am interested in the nature
of blasphemy while having no intention
          of blaspheming. Such issues of respect
          dominate my thinking even when I suffer
vertigo, which is frequently. I'd like to imagine
I can tune into the frequency of leaves
          while they're still clinging, while the last
          conversation between sunlight and cells,
sap and twig or branchlet are taking place.
An outsider inculcating themselves
          into the fate of trees, an xylologist
          of the figurative who is seen
as a threat to mythologies, a blasphemer.

Mildew on the Whiteness of Hölderlin

Mildew on the whiteness of Hölderlin's
shoulders, his phantom limb reaching
towards an ideal he's sure he'll reach.

When the snow comes, I am not even
sure if we'll still be here, and what state
the snow will present in — a white

dusting on mildew, a statement
of collected works in the bookshop
with its limited stock of lyrics.

Hölderlin Old Burse Ghosting

It *had to be* between
the tower and old burse
in willow-inflected
morning river light
that I ghosted
my skin.

I sit unable
to move and he flows
into me —
a cloche.

His metrics are off
but his imagery
intense with the new
blazing summer.

He forgets that I remember
the signature of sparrows
centuries-old
holding out
till the harlequin river
is completely
lost.

Love spreads
via plane trees
and I study
the scene like old
fading negatives
handing them back
to the greening
sun, and briefly
glimpsing
our portraits.

Hölderlin Tower Pride

Weeping willows
don't have predetermined
dispositions, whatever
a past tells them.

They are not weeping
into the green river
a weeping green
any more than
they are drawing
on green as revival.

They are above
and below the water
and hold both tower
and Neckar island
in their layers.

I saw Hölderlin
watching from a window
as the Pride march
wove its way past.
He tapped
on the glass, smiled
green refractions.

Weeping willows,
the deadly heat
of these summers,
but also a joyful love.

He would have walked with us
I think — weeping willows
only gently holding
him back.

Back with Hölderlin, He Takes Me into His Head, *I think*
and thinking over 'Der Spaziergang' ('The Walk')

I look for him again,
but the tower is behind me.

A mallard is at my feet
looking for nourishment,

trying to make me feel relevant.
I realise the river is singing,

relieved at no longer
having to flow towards

a thirsty reactor,
though with notes of sadness

as the residues will persist.
And then he, Hölderlin,

is back with me, offering
access to his head —

a pollarded stump
on the island's southern

bank, sprouting
lashes for spring,

naming with every
wave of its wands.

STATEMENT

Climate change has exposed the misnomers
around 'instinct'. This statement
was gonged by a black woodpecker
in a delimbed, red-lined pine tree
stretching further than heaven or satellites.

A slow worm, discouraged from sliding
onto a pathway where cyclists stress
time over context, was an adaptation,
according to the signature of its tail.

These choices on the day of my father's
funeral in another hemisphere.
This digital brain can't *get* such disjunctions
in order. There was no streaming
facility for the ceremony.

The woodpecker's red-flashed pate
signalled an area —
it was on the far side
of the forest block. My father

grew up in tall jarrah forests,
but so many of those trees were felled.
Tall trees are felled here too. And I saw
an Eurasian Jay sitting on a seat
built by humans for humans,

but there was no human
there to claim and occupy.
Not in that moment.

GHOST CHANTS

(i)

An electric, self-propelled lawn-mower
operates in and out of shade
of an overcast day

on the contained lawn,
almost bumping, riding
roughshod.

You might guess
what I am reading,
wondering about wisteria
in that neighbour's garden,
and processing
those swirling trunks
of my earlier
confusion.

An overcast day,
it operates in and out of shade.
An electric self-propelled lawn-mower.

(ii)

I fear for the forest animals
under the squint
of those hunting lookouts.

Dusk and dawn.
Points of emergence.

The talk of ghosts
before they are even
created.

(iii)

Drawing glasshouses
I have yet to visit
is a mode of interpreting
shadows:
                    a new understanding
that shadows
aren't greyscale
but a range of colours,
if not a full spectrum,
a suppressed version
trying to break
the containment field
of botany.

(iv)

If I walk without studying the path,
only concentrating on the shape
of tall trees' crowns, I won't find

my way through the forest.

Untrue.

Spirals. Spread. Columns. Fountains.
Trigonometric variations. And the cartography
of shyness, its fractures.

(v)

The singer from Placebo has a dispiriting voice.
But there's also something liberating about it.
Imagine the hauntings, and the points
of contact. Imagine the shades of reference.

(vi)

Swallows wave the ear tufts
of dense wheat crops — sometimes
            parting the waters, sometimes
            arising from junctures
within. Gathering insects
to calibrate
                  an agrometeorology.

(vii)

Melancholy descriptors
            make tendrils unravel
as you pass wisteria.

But these tendrils are not
            from wisteria whose
mauve flower heads are failing.

They are jolts. Remembrances.

(viii)

This ghost of myself
will reinterpret conditions
under different guises —

a haze that obscures its buildings,
forests that look large and off-green
but have been cored. Towers.

And critical editions of *Hamlet*
plentiful in the confines
of the town's second-hand store.

Across the barriers, the different
readings of leafy folios.

(ix)

Hay-cut field: round bales
surrounded by many grey herons,
while numerous raptors sweep
          the field of vision.

(x)

I searched out the ghost of a subculture
from decades ago and found a clash

of symbols: the anarchism of Crass
vs. the punk of the UK Subs

who were accused of deeply betraying
their anti-fascist roots but defended

themselves vehemently. The clash
was complicated by an e-scooter

parked in front of the graffiti —
you'd swear the T-bar

was angled for the shot.

(xi)

Are we venting atmosphere
while gravity turns
its attention
to the trajectory
of projectiles, the stress
on the curve of the earth?

(xii)

The Eiffel Tower is not a shepherdess,
nor a shepherd. History lives in its
steel and rivets. The temptation
to add lines would remake a pastoral
we don't need out here, don't want.

(xiii)

Remediating
damaged land — power station
residue — is an investment
in syntax.
                In the reed beds
a tall bird breaks down:
a chemical history
of wavers.

(xiv)

As I inhabit a minor arcana,
you can't expect me
to take myself
less seriously —

evidence from the forest
under threat,
signs of insects flaking
on a glasshouse
roof.

I overhear the semi-arid,
and ignore the distant
electric
self-propelled
lawnmower.

DENDROLOGY OF LIGHTNING

tangents

Hypertangential is a word I've coined
to cope with poems so off-theme

they make you reconsider the very
nature of a theme. Lightning

is hypertangential, kills people,
animals, trees. It rewires.

Remorse isn't something
to construct at a tangent.

I am writing about the agency
of animals and, as if I've

nothing to do with this,
passing it on under

heavy clouds undercircled
by kites and buzzards.

hypographs

Lightning striking a tree
forces vertices of moisture

into hypographs. Flashing
out into immediate surroundings,

heat and shock. Even roots
dead set, ground hum.

Branches snap and trunks
burst. Here, in the state

with the greatest intensity
of strikes. Those points

withheld from the graph,
or on the forest canopy.

Outside, the warning zone's
domain splays across a radar,

an epigraph of loss that reflects
days back, days forward.

lament

Swarms and cascades
of strikes destroying nests

and hollows, no choice
but the odds it will find

an easier way down-up-
through, no chance

for feather or fur to dash
and crash position

on a flat stretch.
In the buildup, stress

like a child grizzling
when teething. I still see

the twice 1 billion joules
of energy that sent me down

this path when I was nine.
A person died from a lightning

strike not far from here
only last week — it is necessary

to remember this,
that beech can be sparked

as much as oak, to record
a deadly side effect

of sheltering,
of dendrology.

PANTHEISM ISM

Have you reckon'd that the landscape took substance and form
that it might be painted in a picture?
Or men and women that they might be written of, and songs sung?
Or the attraction of gravity, and the great laws and harmonious
combinations and the fluids of the air, as subjects for the
savans?
Or the brown land and the blue sea for maps and charts?
Or the stars to be put in constellations and named fancy names?
Or that the growth of seeds is for agricultural tables, or agricul-
ture itself?

Walt Whitman, from 'A Song for Occupations'

(i)

I am losing the landscape but finding the land.
I have filed away the maps and won't be looking
again any time soon. Ploughshares are weapons,
and fields are sown with guns. I am immersed in juxtapositions
I overly hope will lead me astray. I overlay and underlay, sketch
before blocking in. A leaf stuck to my skin forms a new vein pattern.
My biology was never stable. It has never been confirmed that I am
human.
Experimenting with soil, I ignored the strata and watched the bacteria.
Nothing is separable. Declarations like that popped up all over the place.
The place was an insecurity I embedded into observations of weather.

The only name I apply to lacewings are interstices which bounce back
like incomplete sentences. I am less fair to my better self.
Worship is simply a recognition of maxims: axiom, byword, aphorism.
Here I am teaching qualities of quietness and loudness and hoping
the warmth of stones is issued by their own choice. All of this by way
of a narrative I can reread without discovery: all of it will be new.
New is a word I find difficult to say. It is a glitch when I read it repeatedly.
They deliver town planning then take it away. They impose
town planning expecting us to buy into displays. Fire bugs are charting
new paths across the pheromones, their movement noises as familiar
as the hurdy-gurdy. The question isn't who is cranking the handle,
but what kind of paint are the climate protesters using? The provenance
of the pencils I draw into futures. Glasshouses lit after the shift back
from summertime? How will we work through those issues?
We could give a talk on harmony which would really be about inequality.

(ii)

cavillers or questioners

Currer Bell, *Jane Eyre*

The feasibility of singing on a quiet day takes me back to undoing the epic.
The super redness of the tree before it drops all life is not a commentary
on ephemerality. I am permanent in the tree's moment, which is so
obviously
a ploy of language. Speaking as entitled to leaf press and later (much later)

recover its vigour. An adversary to implications of my own body, I unravel
transcriptomes from signwriting out front: messenger molecules
summarising their presence while I present myself as resistance,
not knowing where to duck and cover. Whitman would have talked
about inter-
linking beauty and flow, and delivery and deliverance of genes,
wouldn't he?
Maybe about delivery or deliverance, would have raved on about
all those leaving the building under different guises, stepping
out to join us at the bus stop, travelling slowly to the protest. This melange
of altitudes. The raptor above doesn't work in circles but quadrilaterals.
I stand in the harsh rain between building project noises and silent offices.
On carbon wings, visionaries lift over the violet observatory which glows
like a nightclub.

(iii)

They do and don't want to discover Ultima Thule. Each strike-thru
of others, each blue pencil across grinding horizons. Reduced to language
of drones and interdiction, to deluge and excoriation, the labours
of deletion. Reversing the constitution, walking across fields to the
beacon
of a glasshouse brooding against forest. Backdrop and elision. Where
I trial the painting of scenery they trial new inoculations,
where we bump into the wall of a maze that wasn't there until recently,
where windows are mirrors and scaffolding a dose of introspection.

I was streamed in school and fell with the edges, or walked over the endings:
a plank into performance, a gift to the subscribers. The trees would
        drop their limbs *or* offer shade. I thought it was an equation
        and that I was one of the expressions. I already feared
being embroiled in a form of imperialism, counting the strokes of large
    birds.
I am affected by underlining in red even as I try to ignore its bristling at
    coinages.

(iv)

That glasshouse between houses and forest, snugged into fields,
        emanates hot light, insists on a story beyond transpiration.
        It suggests that a day darkens even before we are willing
to race the clock, and tired tractors flop home on shoes of dead mud.
        The field drops on the inclines, a soft demi-green velveteen deception,
        and the glasshouse light anti-beacons, a repellent but not
a lighthouse this far inland, a dystopia of shorelines and lanterns.
        Some people will fear losing the earlier stars, but others won't
        notice. Not 'won't *even* notice', just not notice. Stars claim us, we don't
claim stars — a statement that doesn't work, though I will die somewhere.
        The glasshouse fire is a growing experiment, an experiment in growth.
        This furious imagination of vegetal embodiment, the rise of plant
            zombies
from glass panels, the racy shadows of leafery and indents of tubers.

(v)

How can I walk knowing such early fire bans are in place where I come from
and don't come from, that *the conditions* will trouble the troubled,
    that the indifferent will cast their burning cigarettes into the tinder?
    Each new placement displaces the contrary voices and nothing is
      addressed
on aerials or dishes. Most the perches are now invisible, or spikes prevent
landings. I am telling the blankness how my life will slip into a photovoltaic
    receptivity, a particular anxiety around tektites and hailstones. Art will
    by illustration over absorption. Dust and mildew, the correlatives
between organic and inorganic variables; who will spring up between.

How can we talk over the drop in auxin and the increasing tendency
    to branch out, to deny the control of apical meristem, an alternative
    communalism draws in the sunlight and offers shade. Through
      consensus,
we connect segments of days, discuss layers of lore and law, apply
ourselves to mulching the furrows. On our raised bed we love
    in shifting ways, adapting to the changing light. A green lacewing
    on the plasterwork is not a threat to the aphids of rapid eye
      movement.
Catch and release. We rely on Shakespeare to have something to say,
like 'bare ruin'd choirs', though its technically not winter yet.

(vi)

Altering wing density and crispness through softening then brittleness
the flyers see patents amass out of the noxious and barely muster
a swarm by way of response. This is not a new phase of
metamorphosis.
Sea lice in fish farms bobbing for apples, and what am I to say in my shell-like
emptiness, my shallow wave-set where the broken reef has broken
the wavefronts into bits. The sea is in me, concentrating with recall
a deeper inland, a buffer of statements. This long historical novel
written in real time, belonging to no genre and wavering with lines
of supply. Imagine if I stopped reading the palms of reptiles, imagine
if they stopped offering them for me to read. I will tell the ornate
rock dragon in the 'Avon Valley' about the European green lizard
blue throating in the Tübingen botanical gardens. Palms off the hot
path,
held up for me to scry. Generous in so many ways. I learnt how close
our fates entwine, or, rather, had it confirmed. But who will listen
to this science? It should be an AI byte at least — a novelty of
obviousness,
a scaly drug deal's dubious side effect. This transcription of saurian events
might have more hope. I will provide a key, arcana and intemperate
blood.

(vii)

Patent pending for proxy indicators in the glacier core grab
    while the going is going, as jet stream labours and wavers
    and record trawling increases its catch to leave an empty bucket.
Research says. Research tells us. Research indicates. According to research.
A suggestion of syntax, the growth rings of clauses, a leaning
    into the televisual predictions of the clouding eyes of fish and their
        wishes,
    brooding slow storms intensifying, warm sea love, trillions of flippers
synchronise swimming making their own diving platforms. The system
reaches in further and further arguing with buffers, tangling in turbines,
    equivocating around smokestacks. Research suggests. Research shows.
    The research seems to. Conservative ex-politicians might defend
the empire builder building a concrete traversal through a sacred
creek bed, contesting the sacred and insisting on ownership,
    the rule of private property. They might, in the jurisdiction
    of their unimaginative freedom. They might, trashing heritage
laws to implement their laws of occupation. They might conduct
their own research to suit their case, patent pending for proxy indicators.

(viii)

What rights to speak across hemispheres, putting the world out of shape,
moving out of synch with the tilt? Which solar panel package, and how
  much storage? The storm accrues energy. Dissemination says the
    mistletoe
  bird among the sticky fruits. But that is also remembering, a position
of nest building. Genomics buzz in the drear lighting of late offices
  extending into footpaths, and messengers virtue signal against protest.
  What leg and what standing? RNA copyrights burst with creativity
shared out by increments: payment plans, direct debit, swipe charging.

Blue tits are more obvious around the edges of The Basin. Counterpoint?
  Too many queries which the more empirical among us might find
    annoying.
  It is, after all, a regime of cats and bells. Conifers tamp the spirits in
    the mass
Leaf drop — spines and cradles, late mosquitoes and fire salamanders
  between rocks, protocols of moss but no binding testament. Dribs and
    drabs
  of gesture, activism, speech. The body wearing down into test casings.
Lights burning harsh in the glasshouses and palms weathering warmer.
Slashes of carmine through detachment are the welts of a virulent agronomy.

(ix)

Each pilcrow forms a distraction of older bathos while gales
harry the shutters whose provenance is hidden by familiarity;
those teased out plough lines churning soil into compliance,
those barking boustrophedon implants just beyond the outer circle,
and each rounding off a flurry in the life cycle of election — cows
beheaded by feed bars, troughing into udder delivery, ear tags
and nu-crops to rise in market consequence, mirror to the emergence
of generations in accordance, that level of gastronomy pegged
by scripts and secretions. Red leaf here doing flower work
in the construction of a scene which is a subset of sublimity, an aesthetic
ruse. Home fires are burning districts out of house and home, raising
them past germination. Squalled in, vengeance and eversiduous wars
compiling unspeakable variables in the appalling almanac of glasshouses.

(x)

I am weary of typologies and typographies — all those hurt creatures
that struggle along the edges of roads, the broken bundles of the dead.
Curling myself up into minimalism, I concentrate on a single pine
cone.
I remember that a large chunk of my vocabulary arose in trying to
describe

the soft twisting of a wing and its seed down into sand. The pine trees
had replaced forests of marri and jarrah trees, and then they had been
logged and housing estates re-rooted the coastal sand. I watched a
single
winged seed fall and lodge, and then I covered it over, wanting growth
of any sort. I was at the gardens again, seeing the unearthed and unearthing,
the preparation of beds for the wintering. To be replanted. And up here,
the new buildings of the Planck Institute for Intelligent Systems
are being plastered and glassed into place. Vivisections are anonymously
boxed and brought in quietly, the old observatory an omphalos.
Such loneliness in worshipping a vastness, bootlegging *weorthscipe*, cosmologies.

VARIATIONS AFTER CHOICE WORDS FROM DONNE'S 'THE HARBINGER TO THE PROGRESS' ('THE SECOND ANNIVERSARY')

Two souls and two mistletoe birds, and mine (a third) an empty shell
Straining with admiration and love for what I can't quite illustrate, to quell
The green heat of the sandpit shaped by earthmovers' tribute, residence
Moved by attempting to *unmark* stones and swirl sand into a lively bliss
That aspires to see the balance sheet as the artwork of a tree
Grown fast on world's last day, the glory of a horticulture degree:
Like as those stars with earth-like planets sold as hope beyond hope, far
Away in the school imagination, *in place*, and waiting for we, the inheritors:
Souls bending at the speed of light, the luggage of human dismay
Burning up as each stage is shed, leaving the curate's egg, halfway
To heaven or eternity, which grows as Π grows, that will outgo
Aspiration of leafage, slow lightning interrupting the flow
Of art as high as the latest batch of meth will allow, blown
As heaven's thinktank; to build on what you can possess, copyright, own;
Can describe as lovingly as you would a pet, or relate
Privately within the safe zone of journals that blessed state?
I envy nothing, especially not the shell of my soul, empty,
Which even when held up to the sun nothing shows, nothing, *see*:
And so, Great Spirit™, what can we trade for lives that hast
Burned you up so fast, what can we bargain for the last
Breath the coal-fired mouths exhale, righteous far, far
Into the night's flesh, wishing upon their lucrative star?
But let's get ethereal, let's wonder at the miracle of flight
Which we highlight as the final birds fly past and out of sight;
Yes, it's that basic, these water-to-wine eyes, God's Phallaceae —

Pisolithus tinctorius which rises out of season, north or south, in its hard
way;
This is it, the *what's here* at our feet, the soul's high progress known
To collapse in a heap when tritium takes possession of its own
Half-life, dye-blooded cows in a paddock, the world's carcass mounted
high
In the government office, in the developer's penthouse, that pure
immortality;
I share with you in a secular light my aspiring thoughts and raise
A few issues that might not seem *seemly*, not worthy of praise;
But it's what I have to offer, and every year
We make new progress, I pick up the pieces to assemble text *here*;
[click link]
And the portfolio grows — the maker's self-praise,
Honour one's insights, one's contributions, and collect one's lays.
And as the broken architecture of Aleppo shrouds
The guilt that sees us fuel our cars and head out under clouds,
Those glorious sainted souls assure us they're operating in our interest,
know
That they are, know the world is large enough to cope, our images below
Those event horizons, those songs we stream to decorate the best
Moments, the worst moments, the soundtrack that makes us blessed?

SELF-SCRUTINY?

No amount of work will make my body better
and this has nothing to do with cosmetics;
the posters over my skin announce an event
I won't be attending, and the ringneck
parrots gambol just above my head, if not
quite in equilibrium. I demand so much
by way of balance, call & response, suggestions
if not answers, and my chatter is a string
of half thoughts, sayings, and alternative
names for subject-object relations — trees
figure large in the shadows of my sleep.

No amount of work will make me more responsive,
though I take as much in as I can, unravelling
image as words later, a confusion of rebus
and gapfill, the Cloze test I answer as the way I see,
not doubting their commitment, determination.
A consequence of squeezing rhythms into shape
is a run down the block where bees 'attack'
and I snap a ligament, but that's retrospective,
and in retrospect lines take shape and warble.
The tin cans on top of star-pickets mess with an
inclination to lightning-spark — they once held legumes.

No amount of work will alleviate the pain,
so I try to build something out of it, the syntax

of pain. But I do not *believe* in pain per se, and refuse
its warnings, but there it is, and there I am,
composing a garden that I am too unwell to replant.
And. the. heat! I say to the paper wasp, that I
have no interest in sin & contracts, and it
tells me it has its own agenda, and that I shouldn't
judge myself so lightly — there's always a past
to fall back into, and the future is a nest
that requires a resolute peduncle, a point of connection
from which to suspend the future of eggs,
the futurelessness of pulped caterpillars.

ENCRYPTION

Phrases attach to events: studying
those rusty wire diamonds of a gate
that looks like the bedstead it could be,
vertical sleep a fence for the garden, a keeping
out which locates an ethics of feeding
without 'containment', insects, reptiles
and birds move through or over. Is
this a statement about exclusion
of mammals or on hot air cryogenics?
Question the question, store your
information in a different seedbank;
the husk of an extra layer of protection.
When we see such massive machinery,
we know how vulnerable art to nature
and nature to art correlations can be,
and we weep in a way that attracts
a variety of insects who breed fast
against the menace of illustration
and edifice, including those forgotten
    nectar-eating mosquitoes.

LIMITATIONS OF PROGRESS

Compacted, will it expand later?
The *hors-texte* threatens to fill or refill
against the bargain basement. The plant operator
has a history contrary to the layers of a road
building up to landscaping, especially as landscape
is what drew cartographers to name features
of terrain against their naming. Even under
the endemic trees, we can probably detect *progress*
by temperament and without assistance,
which is arrogant, but needs must.

This ghost is a lifetime of contradiction,
but not out and out trashing, it hopes. Word-
shifts of leaves and meaning, and grand houses
denying their lawns are an affront, a carpet
of civilising brutality whatever sibilant ironies
are raked from it, whatever moisture beads worked
down into root systems. Compacted, they will spring up
as they move on in their game, following the plays
as it compares its past to its present. *Zany!*

lawn is mowed trim so it reflects the sport
of fighter aircraft doing a flypast, greenly
matching where the roar comes from.

REVENANT

Records clasped onto
as a memorial tree is memorial
for war deaths and also for itself,
is the home base of a magpie clan
scrutinising its options,
one face then many faces
to the world of statues,
of Queen Victoria (Empress of India),
verdigris before uncomfortably
lush trees of generous foliage,
and the colonial godfathery
of Lord Forrest traffic-islanded
to encircle feeding off into features
of botanical casuistry wherein
plant is display above and beyond
while canons bristle and gleam
waiting for next generations;
the sets and subsets of societal
privilege that are powerful engines
hacking the river are in the sails
and mansions that eat away
at the riparian; each retreat of ghost
you set aside will be blocked
by avarice that has made your
ghost what it is, guilt becoming
action then despair at closing

yourself out which assuredly
isn't akin to false pride? Inherent
in the grisly dividing of spoils
is the spoiling of spoils, the dividers
getting antsy over how much
will be left for them and their
going concerns, like Queen Vic's
statue mouthing 'be reasonable',
that engram of transfer: accounts,
ships' manifests, deeds, greenwash
and whitewash, land grants, laundered
and preserved... those substitutes
for ghosts whose life experiences
will stymy delivery, cut access,
besmirch the payoff, muddy
those inheritances of bronze,
Carrara marble, gun metal.

SOAK

Near the head of valley
where a standpipe has been
replaced with a twin-head
fire hydrant riser though
no houses in the valley
have access to scheme
water, in this valley
unto valley, feeding
creek, brook, river —
mantra and more
or less than mantra,
though mantra might be
the wrong word for it,
but it's closer than many
broadacre applications.

Near the head of valley
a soak reshaped to suit
the quadrilateral mode
of rural divisibility,
a soak that gathers
the seep and drainage
of blotter soil for longer
than downhill draws...
aftermath of creek's
opening run, but feeder
of creek's run down to brook,

run tessellated with reeds
which break into patches
around creek's banks, its course,
following the V down,
down where its water
and extra run-off gather,
seep, run and cascade
during a downpour...
and checking the soak
in dry weather holding
its record, I wonder
if it's vaguely possible
that reed warblers
might spontaneously
manifest and nest,
resetting the surveys,
telling truths about water:
clear or murky, still
or flowing, about
vegetation and low flight
such that smallholders
might notice and cherish,
withdraw their fences.

TYPTOLOGY

Each night I occupy
the space between —
as if people won't roam
when others aren't looking,
Yet I am always listening
using the receiver qualities
of the valley. Why do I follow
the odd car in the distance,
or a grain train weaving
down to port? I call
on Latin to translate
bird and mouse, redbacks that favour
night movement, reptiles
knowing the inner resources
of the moon on a hot night.
These rappings on roof
a contraction of corrugated
iron's origin and journey,
as all in the manuscript
is interleafed and consequential.
I have to respond. How many
in sequence and with what
rise and fall? Such intonations
of nightlife far from other houses
of mostly sleeping people.
Waking, those I knew who

are gone and no longer speak
with me. But they appear
when I lapse into sleep
and they are always among
animals and plants. Always
trying to be heard above
many voices, weather conditions,
the irregular workings
of my body, my dismal
          handwriting.

CURING THE GHOST

Curing the ghost
    I catch up
        with the sealing
            of gutters
                three days ago
                    by setting
                        plaster
                            into the wounds
                                of the house planks;
                                    stresses
                                        of an extreme
                                            summer.

Curing the ghost
    so nothing might
        pass through
            its shell.
                Mosquitoes
                    drift in their own
                        shadows
                            though morning sun
                                is already harsh.
                                    This ghost
                                        is a day ghost,
                                            and the cracks
                                                are as diverse
                                                    as lightning,

and will always
be facing
the weather
if left
unsealed.

CODA

A gnat flew close
to the weld-ripple
of fresh plaster
and I feared
it would stick
and be lost
but a gentle puff
through pursed lips
from the side
pushed it away
to continue its
gnat ways.
The plaster
already
curing.

GIVING UP THE GHOST

Copying a text
you introduce
numerous errors
remaking the text
in its own images —
this scraping away
at ground, this
making a platform
on a steep incline
to plant; these
marks of all world's
weight, glib
as complacency,
spending long days
with a foot either
side to keep balance
so the world
doesn't overly
wobble; whose
night and whose
voice and what idiom
do we source, the hounds
on the trail, killed-
off if they can't
keep up the chase,
and if these dogs don't pay
off on their pedigrees?

Who owns the scent,
the chemicals
we have in common
but held in trust
in our skins, shells,
carapaces? You shed
bark from your trunk,
emit globules of sap
from dilated pores;
all of you close
to the surface,
contrite.

TURNING IN ON MY GHOST

Turning in on my ghost
the shortest route is the route
that encounters and traverses
goods and chattels, privacy's
contradictions in terms
of beneficiaries and settled
properties, arriving to where
nature is played off against.

Turning upon my ghost
I reach stands of flooded gums
along the 'winter creek' and plumb
ultra-seasonal truths we could
bring into consideration, though
real estate signage directs
towards niches for love and refusal
of all but stamp duty and rates.

Turning in on my ghost
I garden where dry is far
past wilt, where seed
turns to dust. Scraping
around the house with a shovel,
I make a barrier of disturbed ground,
an irritation of scents and markings
of all that climb or dig to enter.

Turning upon my ghost
I search out cracks and holes,
piercings and apertures,
fearing I will find a way
back into a life that works
for the realtors, providing
them with statistical
evidence of this and that.

Turning in on my ghost
the shortest route is the route
of saying I will do this task
in the morning, first thing,
and keep my word, prove
reliable, and scrawl words
of welcome where they
will most quickly wear away.

Turning in upon my ghost
I will mean those transient
words sincerely, even more
sincerely because of their
pro tem nature, their laxness
in matters of business
investments, of futures,
those nine-tenths of the law.

ACKNOWLEDGEMENTS

I wish to thank Ruth Greenstein, publisher, and Rachael Allen, editor. Thanks to the English Department at the University of Tübingen, with special thanks to Russell West-Pavlov. Tracy Ryan and Tim Kinsella are constant companions in my writing life, and I thank them in all capacities. And thanks to Creative Australia for financial support in the writing of a group of these poems.

I acknowledge that I live on stolen Ballardong Noongar country near Whadjuk Noongar and Yued Noongar countries, and I pay my respect to Noongar culture and its custodians.

Poems collected here have previously appeared in: *Australian Book Review, Eureka Street, Griffith Review, London Magazine, Minimalist: a field journal of mutability and loss* (WA Poets, 2024), *Overland, Plume, Raritan, Remnant: an anthology of microlit* (Spineless Wonders, 2024; ed. Cassandra Atherton), *Smartish Pace, Southern Review, Spoke, Stinging Fly, The Making of a Poem* (Five Islands Press, 2025; ed. Rosanna McGlone), and *The New York Review of Books.*